POPE BENEDICT XVI
PRAYERS

D1296732

United States Conference of Catholic Bishops
Washington, D.C.

Cover photo: Catholic News Service (CNS).

First printing, May 2009

ISBN: 978-1-60137-072-3

CONTENTS

Come, Jesus!
Come and transform the world!
Come today already
and may peace triumph!
Amen!

AUDIENCE
AUGUST 23, 2006

INTRODUCTION

Moments of Prayer*

True prayer is the driving force of the world, since it keeps it open to God.

HOMILY
FEBRUARY 6, 2008

"Those who write to me asking me to pray for them are truly numerous. They tell me of their joys but also their worries, their plans and their family and work problems, the expectations and hopes that they carry in their hearts, together with their apprehensions connected with the uncertainties that humanity is living at the present time. I can assure them that I remember each and every one, especially during the daily celebration of Holy Mass and the recitation of the Rosary. I know well that the principal service I can render to the Church and to humanity is, precisely, prayer, for in praying I confidently place in the Lord's hands the ministry that he himself has entrusted to me, together with the future of the entire ecclesial and civil communities."[1]

"Those who pray never lose hope, even when they find themselves in a difficult and

---

* This Introduction is a collection of Pope Benedict XVI's words compiled from other sources.

even humanly hopeless plight. Sacred Scripture teaches us this and Church history bears witness to this."[2] "When no one listens to me any more, God still listens to me. When I can no longer talk to anyone or call upon anyone, I can always talk to God. When there is no longer anyone to help me deal with a need or expectation that goes beyond the human capacity for hope, he can help me (see *Catechism of the Catholic Church*, no. 2657). When I have been plunged into complete solitude . . . ; if I pray I am never totally alone."[3]

"To pray is not to step outside history and withdraw to our own private corner of happiness. When we pray properly we undergo a process of inner purification which opens us up to God and thus to our fellow human beings as well. In prayer we must learn what we can truly ask of God—what is worthy of God. We must learn that we cannot pray against others. We must learn that we cannot ask for the superficial and comfortable things that we desire at this moment—that meager, misplaced hope that leads us away from God. We must learn to purify our desires and our hopes. We must free ourselves from the hidden lies with which we deceive ourselves. God sees through them, and when we come before God, we too are forced to recognize them . . . This is how we can speak to God and how God speaks to us. In this way we undergo those purifications by which we become open to God and are prepared for the service of our fellow human beings."[4]

"For a Christian, therefore, to pray is not to evade reality and the responsibilities it brings but rather, to fully assume them, trusting in the faithful and inexhaustible love of the Lord."[5] "The Christian who prays does not claim to be able to change God's plans or correct what he has foreseen. Rather, he seeks an encounter with the Father of Jesus Christ, asking God to be present with the consolation of the Spirit to him and his work."[6]

Notes

1 Audience (August 13, 2008).
2 Audience (August 13, 2008).
3 Encyclical *On Christian Hope* (*Spe Salvi*), no. 32.
4 Encyclical *On Christian Hope* (*Spe Salvi*), no. 33.
5 Angelus (March 4, 2007).
6 Encyclical *God Is Love* (*Deus Caritas Est*), no. 37.

PRAYERS
TO GOD

To the Lord

Lord,
make us sensitive to your presence,
help us to hear you,
not to be deaf to you,
help us to keep our hearts free,
open to you.

SPEECH
OCTOBER 3, 2005

For Those Who Are Far from Home

Let us pray to the Lord
that in all of us this desire,
this openness to God,
will be reawakened,
and that even those who do not know Christ
may be touched by his love
so that we are all together on the pilgrimage
to the definitive City,
and that the light of this City may appear
also in our time and in our world. Amen.

AUDIENCE
NOVEMBER 30, 2005

Eucharistic Prayer

Let us pray to the Lord that he will help us
to understand this marvelous mystery
ever more profoundly,
to love it more and more,
and in it, to love the Lord himself ever more.
Let us pray that he will increasingly draw us
   to himself
with Holy Communion.
Let us pray that he will help us
not to keep our life for ourselves
but to give it to him and thus to work
   with him
so that people may find life:
the true life which can only come from
the One who himself is the Way,
the Truth and the Life. Amen.

HOMILY
APRIL 5, 2007

To the Holy Spirit

"Lava quod est sordidum,
riga quod est aridum,
sana quod est saucium.
Flecte quod est rigidum,
fove quod est frigidum,
*rege quod est devium."**

Let us invoke him
so that he will irrigate, warm and straighten,
so that he will pervade us
with the power of his sacred flame
and renew the earth.
Let us pray for this with all our hearts
at this time, in these days.
Amen.

HOMILY
NOVEMBER 7, 2006

---

* From the Pentecost Sequence, *Veni, Sancte Spiritus*: "Heal our
wounds, our strength renew; / on our dryness pour your dew; / wash
the stains of guilt away; / bend the stubborn heart and will; / melt
the frozen, warm the chill; / guide the steps that go astray."

PRAYERS
TO MARY

Prayer of Thanksgiving

Yes, we want to thank you,
Virgin Mother of God
and our most beloved Mother,
for your intercession
for the good of the Church.
You, who in embracing the divine will
    without reserve
were consecrated with all of your energies
to the person and work of your Son,
teach us to keep in our heart
and to meditate in silence, as you did,
upon the mysteries of Christ's life.

May you who reached Calvary,
ever-deeply united to your Son
who from the Cross gave you as mother
to the disciple John,
also make us feel you are always close
in each moment of our lives,
especially in times of darkness and trial.
You, who at Pentecost,
together with the Apostles in prayer,

called upon the gift of the Holy Spirit
for the newborn Church,
help us to persevere in the faithful following
   of Christ.
To you, a "sign of certain hope and comfort,"
we trustfully turn our gaze
"until the day of the Lord shall come"
   (*Lumen Gentium*, no. 68).

You, Mary, are invoked with the
   insistent prayer
of the faithful throughout the world
so that you, exalted above all the angels
   and saints,
will intercede before your Son for us,
"until all families of peoples,
whether they are honored with the title
   of Christian
or whether they still do not know the Savior,
may be happily gathered together in peace
   and harmony
into one People of God,
for the glory of the Most Holy
and Undivided Trinity"
   (*Lumen Gentium*, no. 69). Amen!

PRAYER
DECEMBER 8, 2005

To Mary

Holy Mary, Mother of God,
you have given the world its true light,
Jesus, your Son—the Son of God.
You abandoned yourself completely
to God's call
and thus became a wellspring
of the goodness which flows forth from him.
Show us Jesus. Lead us to him.
Teach us to know and love him,
so that we too can become
capable of true love
and be fountains of living water
in the midst of a thirsting world.

GOD IS LOVE (DEUS CARITAS EST), NO. 42
DECEMBER 25, 2005

Before the Mariensäule in Munich

Holy Mother of the Lord!

Your Son, just before his farewell to
  his disciples,
said to them:
"Whoever wishes to become great among you
must be your servant,
and whoever wishes to be first among you
must be slave of all" (Mk 10:43-44).

At the decisive hour in your own life,
    you said:
"Here I am, the servant of the Lord"
    (Lk 1:38).
You lived your whole life as service.
And you continue to do so
    throughout history.
At Cana, you silently and discreetly interceded
for the spouses,
and so you continue to do.
You take upon yourself people's needs
    and concerns,
and you bring them before the Lord,
before your Son.
Your power is goodness. Your power
    is service.

Teach us—great and small alike—
to carry out our responsibilities in the
    same way.
Help us to find the strength
to offer reconciliation and forgiveness.
Help us to become patient and humble,
but also free and courageous,
just as you were at the hour of the Cross.
In your arms you hold Jesus,
the Child who blesses,
the Child who is also the Lord of the world.
By holding the Child who blesses,

you have yourself become a blessing.
Bless us, this city and this country!
Show us Jesus, the blessed fruit of
   your womb!
Pray for us sinners,
now and at the hour of our death.
Amen!

PRAYER
SEPTEMBER 9, 2006

To Mary

Holy Mary,
Mother of God,
pray for us
so that we may live the Gospel.
Help us not to hide
the light of the Gospel
under the bushel of our meager faith.
Help us by virtue of the Gospel
to be the light of the world,
so that men and women may see goodness
and glorify the Father
who is in Heaven (see Mt 5:14ff.).
Amen!

HOMILY
DECEMBER 10, 2006

To the Madonna of Loreto

Mary,
Mother of the "Yes," you listened to Jesus,
and know the tone of his voice
and the beating of his heart.
Morning Star, speak to us of him,
and tell us about your journey of
    following him
on the path of faith.

Mary,
who dwelt with Jesus in Nazareth,
impress on our lives your sentiments,
your docility, your attentive silence,
and make the Word flourish
in genuinely free choices.

Mary,
speak to us of Jesus,
so that the freshness of our faith
shines in our eyes and warms the heart
of those we meet,
as you did when visiting Elizabeth,
who in her old age rejoiced with you
for the gift of life.

Mary,
Virgin of the *Magnificat*,
help us to bring joy to the world and,

as at Cana, lead every young person
involved in service of others
to do only what Jesus will tell them.

Mary, look upon the *Agora* of youth,
so that the soil of the Italian Church
will be fertile.
Pray that Jesus, dead and Risen,
is reborn in us,
and transforms us into a night full of light,
full of him.

Mary, Our Lady of Loreto, Gate of Heaven,
help us to lift our eyes on high.
We want to see Jesus, to speak with him,
to proclaim his love to all.

PRAYER
SEPTEMBER 2, 2007

To Our Lady of Aparecida, Brazil

Our Mother, protect the Brazilian and Latin
  American family!
Guard under your protective mantle the
  children of this beloved land that
  welcomes us,
As the Advocate with your Son Jesus, give to
  the Brazilian people constant peace and
  full prosperity,
Pour out upon our brothers and sisters
  throughout Latin America a true missionary
  ardor, to spread faith and hope,
Make the resounding plea that you uttered
  in Fatima for the conversion of sinners
  become a reality that transforms the life of
  our society,
And as you intercede, from the Shrine of
  Guadalupe, for the people of the Continent
  of Hope, bless its lands and its homes,
Amen.

SPEECH
MAY 12, 2007

Before the Mariensaüle of Vienna

Holy Mary, Immaculate Mother
of our Lord Jesus Christ,
in you God has given us
the model of the Church
and of genuine humanity.
To you I entrust the country of Austria
and its people.
Help all of us to follow your example
and to direct our lives
completely to God!
Grant that, by looking to Christ,
we may become ever more like him:
true children of God! Then we too,
filled with every spiritual blessing,
will be able to conform ourselves more fully
to his will and to become
instruments of his peace
for Austria, Europe and the world. Amen.

PRAYER
SEPTEMBER 7, 2007

Hail, Star of the Sea

Holy Mary,
Mother of God, our Mother,
teach us to believe,
to hope, to love with you.
Show us the way to his Kingdom!
Star of the Sea,
shine upon us
and guide us on our way!

ON CHRISTIAN HOPE (SPE SALVI), NO. 50
NOVEMBER 30, 2007

Star of Hope

Teach us, Mary,
to believe, to hope, to love with you;
show us the way that leads to peace,
the way to the Kingdom of Jesus.
You, Star of Hope, who wait for us anxiously
in the everlasting light
of the eternal Homeland, shine upon us
and guide us through daily events,
now and at the hour of our death. Amen!

SPEECH
DECEMBER 8, 2007

To Our Lady of Sheshan (Help of Christians)

Virgin Most Holy, Mother of the Incarnate
  Word and our Mother,
venerated in the Shrine of Sheshan under the
  title "Help of Christians,"
the entire Church in China looks to you with
  devout affection.
We come before you today to implore your
  protection.
Look upon the People of God and, with a
  mother's care, guide them
along the paths of truth and love, so that they
  may always be
a leaven of harmonious coexistence among
  all citizens.

When you obediently said "yes" in the house
  of Nazareth,
you allowed God's eternal Son to take flesh in
  your virginal womb
and thus to begin in history the work of
  our redemption.
You willingly and generously cooperated in
  that work,
allowing the sword of pain to pierce
  your soul,

until the supreme hour of the Cross, when
you kept watch on Calvary,
standing beside your Son, who died that we
might live.

From that moment, you became, in a
new way,
the Mother of all those who receive your Son
Jesus in faith
and choose to follow in his footsteps by
taking up his Cross.
Mother of hope, in the darkness of Holy
Saturday you journeyed
with unfailing trust towards the dawn
of Easter.
Grant that your children may discern at
all times,
even those that are darkest, the signs of God's
loving presence.

Our Lady of Sheshan, sustain all those
in China,
who, amid their daily trials, continue to
believe, to hope, to love.
May they never be afraid to speak of Jesus to
the world,
and of the world to Jesus.
In the statue overlooking the Shrine you lift
your Son on high,

offering him to the world with open arms in a
   gesture of love.
Help Catholics always to be credible
   witnesses to this love,
ever clinging to the rock of Peter on which the
   Church is built.
Mother of China and all Asia, pray for us,
   now and for ever. Amen!

SPEECH
MAY 15, 2008

PRAYERS FOR THE SEASONS

For Advent

Mary,
Virgin of expectation and Mother of hope,
revive the spirit of Advent
in your entire Church,
so that all humanity may start out anew
on the journey towards Bethlehem,
from which it came,
and that the Sun that dawns upon us
from on high
will come once again to visit us (see Lk 1:78),
Christ our God. Amen.

HOMILY
DECEMBER 1, 2007

For the Night of Christmas

Let us ask the Lord
to grant us the grace
of looking upon the crib this night
with the simplicity of the shepherds,
so as to receive the joy
with which they returned home (see Lk 2:20).
Let us ask him to give us the humility and
   the faith
with which St. Joseph looked upon the child
that Mary had conceived by the Holy Spirit.
Let us ask the Lord to let us look upon him
with that same love with which Mary
   saw him.
And let us pray that in this way
the light that the shepherds saw will shine
   upon us too,
and that what the angels sang that night
will be accomplished throughout the world:
"Glory to God in the highest,
and on earth peace among men with whom
   he is pleased."
Amen!

HOMILY
DECEMBER 24, 2006

For the New Year

Dear brothers and sisters,
at the beginning of this new year
let us revive within us the commitment
to open our minds and hearts to Christ,
sincerely showing him our desire
to live as his true friends. . . .
May Mary help us open our hearts
to the Emmanuel
who took on our poor, weak flesh
in order to share with us
the arduous journey of earthly life.
In the company of Jesus, however,
this tiring journey becomes a joyful journey.
Let us proceed
together with Jesus,
let us walk with him
and thus the new year will be a happy and
    good year.

AUDIENCE
JANUARY 3, 2007

For Lent

Dear brothers and sisters,
may the Lenten Season . . .
be a renewed experience
of the merciful love of Christ,
who poured out his Blood for us on
    the Cross.
Let us docilely attend his school,
to learn in turn to "give anew"
his love to our neighbors,
especially those who are suffering and
    in difficulty.
This is the mission of every disciple of Christ,
but to carry it out it is essential to continue
    listening to his Word
and to be assiduously nourished by his Body
    and his Blood.
May the Lenten journey,
which in the ancient Church was a journey
    towards Christian initiation,
towards Baptism and the Eucharist,
be a "Eucharistic" Season for us
in which we participate with greater fervor
in the Eucharistic Sacrifice.
May the Virgin Mary,
who after sharing in the sorrowful Passion
of her divine Son

experienced the joy of his Resurrection,
accompany us during this Lent
towards the Mystery of Easter,
the supreme Revelation of God's Love.

AUDIENCE
FEBRUARY 21, 2007

For the Paschal Vigil

Lord, show us
that love is stronger than hatred,
that love is stronger than death.
Descend into the darkness
and the abyss of our modern age,
and take by the hand those who await you.
Bring them to the light!
In my own dark nights, be with me to bring
   me forth!
Help me, help all of us, to descend with you
into the darkness of all those people
who are still waiting for you,
who out of the depths cry unto you!
Help us to bring them your light!
Help us to say the "yes" of love,
the love that makes us descend with you
and, in so doing, also to rise with you.
Amen!

HOMILY
APRIL 7, 2007

For Pentecost

Let us pray to God the Father, therefore,
through Our Lord Jesus Christ,
in the grace of the Holy Spirit,
so that the celebration of the Solemnity
    of Pentecost
may be like an ardent flame and a
    blustering wind
for Christian life
and for the mission of the whole Church.

HOMILY
JUNE 3, 2006

For the Assumption

Mary,
while you accompany us
in the toil of our daily living and dying,
keep us constantly oriented
to the true homeland of bliss.
Help us to do as you did.

Help us, Mother,
bright Gate of Heaven,
Mother of Mercy,
source through whom came Jesus Christ,
our life and our joy. Amen.

HOMILY
AUGUST 15, 2008

PRAYERS FOR THE CHURCH

For the Kingdom of God

Let us be yours, Lord [Jesus]!
Pervade us, live in us;
gather scattered humanity
in your body,
so that in you everything may be
subordinated to God
and you can then hand over the universe
to the Father, in order that
"God may be all in all" (1 Cor 15:28).

JESUS OF NAZARETH, P. 147

Prayer of the Body of the Lord

Lord,
guide us on the paths of our history!
Show the Church and her Pastors
again and again the right path!
Look at suffering humanity,
cautiously seeking a way through so
    much doubt;
look upon the physical and mental hunger
    that torments it!
Give men and women bread for body
    and soul!
Give them work! Give them light!
Give them yourself!
Purify and sanctify all of us!
Make us understand
that only through participation in
    your Passion,
through "yes" to the cross, to self-denial,
to the purifications that you impose upon us,
our lives can mature
and arrive at true fulfillment.
Gather us together from all corners of
    the earth.
Unite your Church,
unite wounded humanity!
Give us your salvation! Amen!

HOMILY
JUNE 15, 2006

Pray for Me

Pray for me,
that I may learn to love the Lord more
   and more.
Pray for me,
that I may learn to love his flock more
   and more—
in other words, you, the holy Church,
each one of you and all of you together.
Pray for me, that I may not flee for fear of
   the wolves.
Let us pray for one another,
that the Lord will carry us
and that we will learn to carry one another.

HOMILY
APRIL 24, 2005

For John Paul II

"Wait for the Lord;
be strong, and let your heart take courage;
yes, wait for the Lord!" (Ps 27 [26]:13-14).
Yes, let your heart take courage,
dear brothers and sisters, and burn
   with hope! . . .
May the *Totus tuus* of the beloved Pontiff
encourage us to follow him
on the path of the gift of ourselves to Christ
through the intercession of Mary,
and may she herself,
   the Virgin Mary,
obtain it for us
while we entrust to her motherly hands
this father, brother and friend of ours,
that he may rest in God and rejoice in peace.
Amen.

HOMILY
APRIL 2, 2007

The Prayer of Pope Leo the Great

"Pray to our good God
that in our day he will be so good
as to reinforce faith, multiply love
and increase peace.
May he render me, his poor servant,
adequate for his task
and useful for your edification,
and grant me to carry out this service
so that together with the time given to me
my dedication may grow.
Amen."

QUOTED IN HOMILY
APRIL 15, 2007

For Vocations

O Father, raise up among Christians
abundant and holy vocations to
   the priesthood,
who keep the faith alive
and guard the blessed memory
   of your Son Jesus
   through the preaching of his word
and the administration of the Sacraments,
with which you continually renew
   your faithful.

Grant us holy ministers of your altar,
who are careful and fervent guardians
   of the Eucharist,
   the sacrament of the supreme gift of Christ
for the redemption of the world.

Call ministers of your mercy,
who, through the sacrament
   of Reconciliation,
spread the joy of your forgiveness.

Grant, O Father, that the Church may
  welcome with joy
the numerous inspirations of the Spirit of
  your Son
and, docile to His teachings,
may she care for vocations to the
  ministerial priesthood
and to the consecrated life.
Sustain the Bishops, priests and deacons,
consecrated men and women, and all the
  baptized in Christ,
so that they may faithfully fulfill their mission
at the service of the Gospel.

This we pray through Christ our Lord. Amen.

Mary, Queen of Apostles, pray for us!

MESSAGE
MARCH 5, 2006

Stay with Us

Stay with us, Lord,
keep us company,
even though we have not always
    recognized you.
Stay with us, because all around us
the shadows are deepening,
and you are the Light;
discouragement is eating its way into
    our hearts:
make them burn with the certainty of Easter.
We are tired of the journey,
but you comfort us in the breaking of bread,
so that we are able to proclaim to our
    brothers and sisters
that you have truly risen
and have entrusted us with the mission
of being witnesses of your resurrection.

Stay with us, Lord,
when mists of doubt, weariness or difficulty
rise up around our Catholic faith;
you are Truth itself, you are the one who
    reveals the Father to us:
enlighten our minds with your word,
and help us to experience the beauty of
    believing in you.

SPEECH
MAY 13, 2007

For Young People

Let us turn our gaze, our eyes,
once again to Mary, model of humility
    and courage.
Virgin of Nazareth,
help us to be docile to the work of the
    Holy Spirit,
as you were;
help us to become ever more holy,
disciples in love with your Son Jesus;
sustain and guide these young people
so that they may be joyful and
    tireless missionaries
of the Gospel among their peers
in every corner of Italy.
Amen!

HOMILY
SEPTEMBER 2, 2007

PRAYERS FOR THE WORLD

Invocation

O Lord,
make your face shine upon us,
for goodness in peace.
In these times,
grant concord and peace to us
and to all the inhabitants of the earth,
through Jesus Christ who reigns
from generation to generation
and for ever and ever. Amen.

AUDIENCE
SEPTEMBER 28, 2005

For Peace (1)

Lord, fulfill your promise!
Where there is conflict,
give birth to peace!
Where there is hatred,
make love spring up!
Where darkness prevails,
let light shine!
Make us heralds of your peace! Amen.

HOMILY
DECEMBER 24, 2005

For Peace (2)

May this be our prayer at this time:
"Free us from every evil
and grant us peace!"
Not tomorrow nor the day after tomorrow:
Lord, give us peace today!
Amen.

SPEECH
JULY 23, 2006

For the Family

Lord,
remain in our families,
enlighten them in their doubts,
sustain them in their difficulties,
console them in their sufferings
and in their daily labors,
when around them shadows build up
which threaten their unity and their
    natural identity.
You are Life itself:
remain in our homes,
so that they may continue to be nests
where human life is generously born,
where life is welcomed, loved and respected
from conception to natural death.

SPEECH
MAY 13, 2007

For the Polish People

Dearest brothers and sisters,
I am asking you to look up from earth
    to heaven,
to lift your eyes to the One
to whom succeeding generations have looked
for two thousand years,
and in whom they have discovered life's
    ultimate meaning.
Strengthened by faith in God,
devote yourselves fervently
to consolidating his Kingdom on earth,
a Kingdom of goodness, justice,
solidarity and mercy.
I ask you to bear courageous witness
to the Gospel before today's world,
bringing hope to the poor, the suffering,
the lost and abandoned, the desperate
and those yearning for freedom, truth
    and peace.
By doing good to your neighbor
and showing your concern for the
    common good,
you bear witness that God is love.

I ask you, finally,
to share with the other peoples of Europe and
  the world
the treasure of your faith,
not least as a way of honoring
the memory of your countryman,
who, as the Successor of St. Peter,
did this with extraordinary power
  and effectiveness.
And remember me in your prayers
  and sacrifices,
even as you remembered my
  great Predecessor,
so that I can carry out
the mission Christ has given me.
I ask you to stand firm in your faith!
Stand firm in your hope!
Stand firm in your love! Amen!

HOMILY
MAY 28, 2006

For the Mission of Secular Life

Dear brothers and sisters, . . .
choose and live the Word of God:
following the example of Mary, let it guide
  your decisions
in the family, at work and in the
  Christian community.
Continue to walk in faith and,
faithful to the mission entrusted to you,
approach all creatures with joy and care
to communicate the gifts of salvation.
Remember that you are part of a history
and a rich tradition of witnesses
faithful to God and to the Gospel.
Be guided by the Holy Spirit
so that you may become leaven for new life,
salt of the earth
and light of the world.
May the blessings of the Lord, who is
  our peace,
be your comfort and consolation.

PRAYER
SEPTEMBER 8, 2007

At Ground Zero in New York

O God of love, compassion, and healing,
look on us, people of many different faiths
    and traditions,
who gather today at this site,
the scene of incredible violence and pain.

We ask you in your goodness
to give eternal light and peace
to all who died here—
the heroic first-responders:
our fire fighters, police officers,
emergency service workers, and Port
    Authority personnel,
along with all the innocent men and women
who were victims of this tragedy
simply because their work or service
brought them here on September 11, 2001.

We ask you, in your compassion
to bring healing to those
who, because of their presence here that day,
suffer from injuries and illness.
Heal, too, the pain of still-grieving families
and all who lost loved ones in this tragedy.
Give them strength to continue their lives
    with courage and hope.

We are mindful as well
of those who suffered death, injury, and loss
on the same day at the Pentagon
and in Shanksville, Pennsylvania.
Our hearts are one with theirs
as our prayer embraces their pain and suffering.

God of peace, bring your peace to our
   violent world:
peace in the hearts of all men and women
and peace among the nations of the earth.
Turn to your way of love
those whose hearts and minds
are consumed with hatred.

God of understanding,
overwhelmed by the magnitude of this tragedy,
we seek your light and guidance
as we confront such terrible events.
Grant that those whose lives were spared
may live so that the lives lost here
may not have been lost in vain.
Comfort and console us,
strengthen us in hope,
and give us the wisdom and courage
to work tirelessly for a world
where true peace and love reign
among nations and in the hearts of all.

PRAYER
APRIL 20, 2008

At the Western Wall

God of all the ages,
on my visit to Jerusalem, the "City of Peace,"
spiritual home to Jews, Christians and
    Muslims alike,
I bring before you the joys, the hopes and
    the aspirations,
the trials, the suffering and the pain of all
    your people throughout the world.

God of Abraham, Isaac and Jacob,
hear the cry of the afflicted, the fearful,
    the bereft;
send your peace upon this Holy Land, upon
    the Middle East,
upon the entire human family;
stir the hearts of all who call upon your name,
to walk humbly in the path of justice
    and compassion.

"The Lord is good to those who wait for him,
to the soul that seeks him" (Lam 3:25)!

PRAYER
MAY 12, 2009

Prayer of Reciprocity

I pray for you:
pray for me too,
so that in all life's problems
we may always be aware
of the Lord's goodness
and thus press on
through difficult days
as well as beautiful ones.
My prayers for you all and my Blessing.

SPEECH
AUGUST 3, 2008

Maranà, Thà

Come, Lord Jesus!
Come in your way,
in the ways that you know.
Come wherever there is injustice and violence.
Come to the refugee camps,
in Darfur, in North Kivu, in so many parts of
the world.

Come wherever drugs prevail.
Come among those wealthy people
who have forgotten you,
who live for themselves alone.
Come wherever you are unknown.
Come in your way
and renew today's world.
And come into our hearts,
come and renew our lives,
come into our hearts
so that we ourselves may become the light
   of God,
your presence.
In this way let us pray with St. Paul:
Maranà, thà! "Come, Lord Jesus!"
And let us pray that Christ may truly
   be present
in our world today
and renew it.
Amen.

AUDIENCE
NOVEMBER 12, 2008